SHAKESPEARE FOR EVERYONE

MACBETH

By Jennifer Mulherin   *Illustrations by* Lesley Scoble

CHERRYTREE BOOKS

Author's note

There is no substitute for seeing the plays of Shakespeare performed. Only then can you really understand why Shakespeare is our greatest dramatist and poet. This book simply gives you the background to the play and tells you about the story and characters. It will, I hope, encourage you to see the play.

A Cherrytree Book

Designed and produced by
A S Publishing

First published 1988
by Cherrytree Press Ltd
a subsidiary of
The Chivers Company Ltd
Windsor Bridge Road
Bath, Avon BA2 3AX

Copyright © Cherrytree Press Ltd 1988

British Library Cataloguing in Publication Data

Mulherin, Jennifer
    Macbeth.——(Shakespeare for everyone).
    1. Shakespeare, William. Macbeth
    I. Title   II. Scoble, Lesley   III. Series
    822.3'3   PR2823

    ISBN 0-7451-5015-2

Printed in Hong Kong by Colorcraft Ltd

Contents

Macbeth *and the English throne*

A martyr being hanged. Many people died for their religion during Shakespeare's time. Some were burned at the stake, or hanged. Others were beheaded.

Macbeth is a play about kingship and a traitor who overthrows the rightful ruler of his country. In the years before Shakespeare's birth and during his lifetime, there were many threats to England's rulers.

Bloody Mary

When Shakespeare was born, Queen Elizabeth I had been on the throne for six years. She had succeeded her sister Mary (the daughter of Henry VIII and Katherine of Aragon), who was a Roman Catholic. Mary had tried to restore Catholicism as the main religion in England. And she persecuted without mercy those people who remained Protestants. Hundreds of people were burned to death at the stake and because of this she was known as 'Bloody Mary'. Only her death saved the country from a rebellion against her bad government and her reign of terror. So when her sister, Elizabeth, who was the daughter of Henry and Anne Boleyn, and a Protestant, came to the throne there was great rejoicing.

Good Queen Bess

England was in a bad state when the young Elizabeth became Queen. The country was almost bankrupt after a disastrous war with France. It had no army or navy and no money to build them. And the religious disputes had left the country unsettled. Some Roman Catholics wanted to continue Mary's work. And some Protestants – the Puritans – wanted an extreme form of Protestantism to be the main religion.

Fortunately, Elizabeth proved to be a strong ruler who did not believe in extremes. She was clever and well-educated. She loved music and dancing and she adored pretty clothes and jewels – as her portraits show. She liked gaiety, laughter and witty people. And she liked to be admired by handsome, young men. But she could also be strong-minded, quick-tempered and stubborn.

However, with the people, she was always straightforward and honest. She was determined to unite the country and give it peace and prosperity. And the people loved her because of her forthright character and her wish to make England great. They called her 'Good Queen Bess'. She was one of the most popular rulers England has ever had. And she did, indeed, make England a powerful and prosperous country.

The Queen who refused to marry
The Queen's advisers were very concerned that she should marry and produce an heir. This was because the next in line to the throne was Mary, Queen of Scots. She was a frivolous, pretty woman who had been brought up in France and was a Roman Catholic. But Elizabeth refused to marry, even though she had a number of 'favourites'. One was the handsome Robert Dudley, Earl of Leicester. The Queen visited his castle at Kenilworth in 1557. This is only 30 miles from Stratford and Shakespeare, aged eleven, might well have been one of the many sightseers who visited the place to get a glimpse of the Queen.

Another of the Queen's favourites was Sir Water Raleigh. He was responsible for the first English voyage to America and he named the land Virginia, after the unmarried Queen. A US state still bears this name.

Queen Elizabeth dancing with her 'favourite', the Earl of Leicester. When the Queen visited the Earl at Kenilworth, it cost £1000 a day to entertain her.

The execution of Mary, Queen of Scots

Mary, Queen of Scots believed that she was the rightful heir to the English throne; and she plotted against Elizabeth all her life. Despite this, Elizabeth tolerated her until her last Catholic plot was uncovered. This was to murder Elizabeth and place herself on the throne with the help of the Catholic King of Spain. Mary was tried and found guilty and executed in 1587.

The defeat of the Spanish Armada

Spain was the most powerful country in the world at that time. It had conquered the New World (North and South America). But Sir Francis Drake had captured many Spanish ships – laden with treasures – on their way home; and this was a threat to Spain's power. Urged on by the Pope, the Spanish King decided to send a fleet of ships – the Armada – to invade England. His aim was to destroy her power and to restore Catholicism to the country. In the great sea battle that followed, the Spanish were defeated. From then on, England grew in wealth and strength.

The rest of Elizabeth's reign was not without its difficulties. There was a revolt in Ireland. And another of the queen's favourites, the Earl of Essex, was the leader of a plot against her. He, like Mary, Queen of Scots, was executed for treason. Elizabeth survived into old age. And future generations looked back on her reign as the golden age of English history.

The new King, James I

The new king was James I, King of Scotland and the son of Mary, Queen of Scots. He was brought up as a Protestant so he was a popular heir to the throne. However, at first, people were not certain how strong a ruler he would be. Because of this, some Roman Catholics, including Guy Fawkes, plotted against him. Shakespeare's play *Macbeth* dwells – in an indirect way – on these threats to the new king's rule.

Macbeth is the story of a man who plotted to overthrow the rightful king. And Shakespeare makes it clear that he is a traitor. But most of the English people were, like Shakespeare, on James's side. And this was the last Catholic threat to the kingdom until the 1680s, long after Shakespeare's death.

James I, the King of Scotland, who succeeded Queen Elizabeth. He was brought up as a Protestant. He was a religious man and rather serious. He had a particular interest in witchcraft.

A new play for a new King

When Shakespeare wrote this play in about 1605 or 1606, King James I had succeeded Elizabeth I on the English throne. Before then, he had been King of Scotland. So Shakespeare in telling this story of one of Scotland's early kings was doing so in order to please James. The King, who was a patron of the arts, had doubled the amount of money paid to the playwright and actors for playing before the Court. Because of this, Shakespeare had good reason to be grateful to him.

Why the story of Macbeth?
In Shakespeare's play, Macbeth is a Scottish nobleman who, because of his ambition to be a king, murders the rightful ruler of Scotland, Duncan. He then kills another nobleman, Banquo, because some witches prophesy that Banquo's descendants will be kings. Now Banquo was said to be the ancestor of the Stuart kings and James, like King Charles I and Charles II, was a Stuart. So in making Banquo a hero in this play, Shakespeare was flattering James and his ancestors and supporting his right to be on the English throne – a view which not everyone agreed with.

The real Macbeth
Macbeth really was a King of Scotland. He ruled in the 1000s and Shakespeare found the story in a history book called *Chronicles of England, Scotland and Ireland* by Ralph

Newes from Scotland.

These pictures, made at the time, show Agnes Sampson and other so-called witches in front of their cauldron (left). *In the background is the ship which, she confessed, she tried to wreck. After being arrested, she was cross-examined by James I himself* (below), *she was found guilty of being a witch and was sentenced to death.*

Holinshed. This book was popular in Shakespeare's day and he took the stories of other kings of England, like Richard III and Henry V, from it. But he often changed some of the facts and added things to make his plays more dramatic and interesting. He did this with Macbeth who, by all accounts, was not quite as evil and wicked as Shakespeare makes him out to be.

Witches and ghosts

Shakespeare put spirits and ghosts in lots of his plays. But in no other play did he make these creatures as horrible and demon-like as the witches in *Macbeth*. Now James I was especially interested in witches because a so-called witch, Agnes Sampson, was supposed to have tried to wreck his ship when he sailed to Denmark to get married. She later confessed this before being condemned to death. Soon after, James wrote a book on witchcraft called *Demonology*.

These two men are being helped by the devil to commit murder. In Shakespeare's time, most people believed that the devil or other evil spirits urged a person on to do wrong.

From it Shakespeare learnt about witches' spells and chants and their ability to see into the future. The fairies, elves and goblins that feature in some of Shakespeare's other plays are mostly good. But these witches are evil – they are creatures of the devil and their prophecies cause Macbeth to commit murder.

The Gunpowder Plot

Treason – when a person or a group of people plot to overthrow the king or government – was on everybody's mind when Shakespeare wrote *Macbeth*. The reason for this was that in November 1605 the Gunpowder Plot had been discovered. Guy Fawkes, along with some other Roman Catholics, got together and planned to blow up the Houses of Parliament. Their aim was to bring down the government and to put a Catholic ruler on the throne. Fortunately, they were found out in time and were tried and killed as traitors.

9

And to this very day, we remember their 'gunpowder, treason and plot' when on November 5th each year we light bonfires on Guy Fawkes Day. Shakespeare, along with most other people in the country, sided with the King. At this time, then, a play about a villainous traitor was very topical. Shakespeare knew that his play would not only please the King but would also be popular with the people. And it was. From that day to this, it has been put on more often than most of Shakespeare's other plays.

The conspirators in the Gunpowder Plot. The plot was kept secret for 18 months. During this time a tunnel was dug under the Houses of Parliament. Here 36 barrels of gunpowder were stored. The plot was only discovered on the day before the gunpowder was to be used.

Creating the mood

Macbeth is a tragedy, a serious story which ends with the death of the main character. Shakespeare tells us how a brave and noble man is changed into a murderer and traitor because of his ambition to become King of Scotland – and how in the end he is defeated and killed by those loyal to the rightful king. The play takes place in Scotland and much of

Three witches depicted as people imagined them in Shakespeare's day. Cats and other animals were supposed to help the witches cast their spells.

it at night. This helps to make the atmosphere more menacing. And Shakespeare creates images in words and effects on stage that keep the audience on the edge of their seats.

The witches seem to appear from nowhere and then disappear – and they dance around a cauldron filled with horrible things. Fogs, mists and wild storms create a threatening atmosphere and the audience shrinks in horror at Macbeth's blood-stained hands. When Banquo's ghost appears, we are as startled and as frightened as Macbeth. When Lady Macbeth walks in her sleep, we share her guilt-ridden nightmare. Shakespeare succeeds in building up a powerful and exciting story. Like a good ghost story, we are still affected by its mood and atmosphere – and by the terrible things that happen – every time we see it on the stage. Most people think it is one of Shakespeare's greatest plays.

This is because, as well as creating an exciting story, he has shown us how a good and noble person – like we all think we are – can be turned into a murderer and a villain.

The story of Macbeth

Meeting the witches
Right at the beginning, Shakespeare sets the mood of the story. There is thunder and lightning and three witches appear. They announce that they will meet again on a heath to greet Macbeth. Then they disappear into the 'filthy air' as mysteriously as they arrived. What terrible things, the audience wonders, will they say to Macbeth?

How brave Macbeth defeats the enemy
Meanwhile, a battle has been going on between soldiers loyal to King Duncan of Scotland and the troops of some rebel Scottish lords. The rebels have been supported in battle by the King of Norway and his soldiers. But, after fierce fights, Duncan's bravest and most loyal general, the noble Macbeth, defeats the enemy. The King learns that one

of the rebel lords, the Thane of Cawdor, has been caught and he orders that he be killed as a traitor. So pleased is the King with Macbeth that he bestows on him the title Thane of Cawdor. And he sends two of his noblemen, Ross and Angus, to greet Macbeth – who is returning from battle – with the news.

Macbeth and Banquo meet the witches

Macbeth is returning from the battle with his friend and fellow nobleman, Banquo. Their journey back to the King's camp takes them over a deserted heath. Here the witches lie in wait for them – talking as they do about the evil spells they have cast on people. The mist clears and Macbeth and Banquo suddenly see the witches. They demand that these creatures 'So wither'd and so wild in their attire', explain who they are. When the witches speak, they greet Macbeth as Thane of Cawdor and prophesy that he will be king. To Banquo they say, 'Your heirs will be kings, although you will not be king.' Then they disappear again. Puzzled and curious, Banquo and Macbeth do not know what to make of the incident.

Macbeth dreams of becoming king

At that moment Ross and Angus arrive. They tell Macbeth that he has been made Thane of Cawdor. Until then Macbeth did not know that Cawdor had been caught and killed. The first prophecy of the witches has come true. And Macbeth begins to think about the second one – that he will be king. Banquo warns him about evil spirits but Macbeth ponders aloud to himself. If, after all, he became Thane of Cawdor by chance, maybe he could also become king. For a moment, he imagines himself killing Duncan. Then he dismisses the horrid thought. We know though that he is now becoming ambitious.

The witches' chant

The Weird Sisters, hand in hand,
Posters of the sea and land,
Thus do go, about, about,
Thrice to thine, and thrice to mine,
And thrice again, to make up nine.

ACT I Sc III

13

Macbeth is honoured with the King's visit

At Duncan's castle, Macbeth and Banquo are warmly welcomed by the King. Duncan announces that he is making one of his sons, Malcolm, heir to the throne. Then he declares that he intends to visit Macbeth at his castle in Inverness. This is a great honour so Macbeth hurries off to prepare for the King's arrival. But as he leaves, he broods about Malcolm – the heir to the throne – and tries to suppress his own evil thoughts.

> **Lady Macbeth on Macbeth's nature**
> *It is too full o' the milk of human kindness*
> *To catch the nearest way: thou wouldst be great,*
> *Art not without ambition, but without*
> *The illness should attend it . . .*
>
> Act I Sc v

Lady Macbeth plans a murder

Meanwhile, at home in their castle in Inverness, Lady Macbeth has received a letter from her husband. In it he tells her about the witches' prophecies.

At that moment a messenger arrives telling her of the King's visit. She realises that this is the golden opportunity to kill the King. She voices her treacherous thoughts to herself, and unlike Macbeth does not try to suppress them. She makes up her mind that the murder must be committed that night. When Macbeth arrives at the castle ahead of the King, she tells him she has arranged everything.

Macbeth has his fears and doubts

Duncan arrives on a beautiful summer's day and Lady Macbeth welcomes him in a most friendly way. Macbeth, however, has been thinking about the murder. He is frightened about what will happen after he kills Duncan. He has doubts about it. Duncan is his cousin and he is a

> **Duncan describes Macbeth's castle**
> *This castle hath a pleasant seat; the air*
> *Nimbly and sweetly recommends itself*
> *Unto our gentle senses.*
>
> Act I Sc vi

good king who is popular with everyone. Macbeth tells himself that there is no reason to kill Duncan – except to satisfy his own ambition to be king. So he tells Lady Macbeth that he has changed his mind.

Lady Macbeth's anger

Lady Macbeth is furious. She accuses him of being a coward for not having the courage to do what he wants. She angrily says that she would kill her own child if that was what she had promised to do. Her feelings are so strong that Macbeth gives in completely. And he agrees to go ahead as she has planned.

Macbeth sees a blood-stained dagger

Banquo is also a guest at the castle. That night he feels uneasy and cannot sleep. He has been thinking of the witches and has a feeling that something terrible is going to happen. Macbeth, too, thinks about the murder. Alone in his room, he has a terrible vision of a dagger which he tries to grasp but cannot get hold of. He tells himself that he is imagining things because he is afraid. But he keeps seeing the dagger – the second time with blood on it. Then he hears a bell ring. This is Lady Macbeth's signal. He now has to kill Duncan.

Macbeth's vision of a dagger

Is this a dagger which I see before me,
The handle towards my hand? Come, let me clutch thee.
I have thee not, and yet I see thee still.
Art thou not, fatal vision, sensible
To feeling as to sight? or art thou but
A dagger of the mind, a false creation,
Proceeding from the heat-oppressed brain?

Act ii Sc vi

> **Macbeth summoned to Duncan's murder**
>
> *I go and it is done: the bell invites me.*
> *Hear it not, Duncan, for it is a knell*
> *That summons thee to heaven, or to hell.*
>
> Act II Sc i

How Macbeth murders Duncan

Lady Macbeth has made sure that Duncan's guards are asleep by putting drugs in their drink. And she has put out two daggers for Macbeth to use. She keeps watch outside while Macbeth enters the King's chambers. When he comes out he is staggering. His arms are covered with blood and he is still holding the blood-stained daggers. It is obvious that Macbeth has gone to pieces. He is overcome by guilt and horror at what he has done. She tells him to pull himself together – to take the daggers back and smear the guards with blood. But Macbeth is in such a state of shock that he cannot. At that moment they hear a loud knocking at the gates of the castle. Lady Macbeth knows that this might awaken the household. She quickly replaces the daggers herself and sends Macbeth to change into his nightgown, so that he can pretend he has been asleep.

> **Macbeth on sleep**
>
> *Methought I heard a voice cry 'Sleep no more!*
> *Macbeth does murder sleep'– the innocent sleep,*
> *Sleep that knits up the ravelled sleave of care,*
> *The death of each day's life, sore labour's bath,*
> *Balm of hurt minds, great Nature's second course,*
> *Chief nourisher in life's feast, –*
>
> Act II Sc ii

17

The horrible deed is discovered

The porter at the gate has been slow to open the gates. He had fallen into a drunken sleep and did not hear the knocking. Eventually he lets in the nobles, Lennox and Macduff. They explain to Macbeth that the King had asked them to call him at a very early hour. While Macduff goes to waken the King, Lennox describes how their night was disturbed by strange sounds and happenings. But just as he finishes speaking, Macduff returns horror stricken. He blurts out that Duncan has been murdered. He rings the alarm bells to wake up the castle while Macbeth rushes off to investigate. Lady Macbeth, Banquo and Duncan's sons hear the news as Macbeth returns. He confesses he has just killed the suspected murderers, the guards, in a fit of rage. Lady Macbeth faints – or pretends to faint – in horror.

> **A disturbed night**
> *The night has been unruly: where we lay,*
> *Our chimneys were blown down, and, as they say,*
> *Lamentings heard i' th' air, strange screams of death,*
> *And prophesying with accents terrible*
> *Of dire combustion and confused events . . .*
>
> Act II Sc iii

Macbeth becomes King of Scotland

Confusion follows with no one knowing what to do. But Duncan's sons, Malcolm and Donalbain, think that if their father was killed, they too are in danger. They decide to flee. But this makes them suspects of the murder so Macbeth is appointed king – just as he wanted.

The new King plans another murder

Not long after he is crowned, Macbeth decides to give a banquet at his castle. He asks Banquo to be guest of honour. But Banquo secretly believes that Macbeth murdered Duncan. On the day of the banquet, Macbeth takes a special interest in how Banquo and his son Fleance are to spend the afternoon. The reason is that Macbeth is afraid of Banquo because of the witches' prophecy. They said, remember, that Banquo's heirs would be kings. In fact Macbeth has arranged to see some hired murderers who are to kill Banquo that afternoon – before the banquet.

Macbeth does not confide in the Queen

Lady Macbeth, meeting her husband after the murderers leave, thinks he is brooding about Duncan's murder. She tries to cheer him up by saying 'what's done, is done.' He asks her to be especially pleasant to Banquo that night. What he does not tell her is that he has already ordered the murder. And, sure enough, as Banquo and Fleance are returning to the castle for the banquet, they are attacked by the murderers. Banquo is killed but Fleance luckily escapes and runs away.

What happens at the banquet

Macbeth learns about Banquo's death and the escape of Fleance just as the banquet begins. Then, as he goes to take his place at the table, he sees the ghost of Banquo sitting in his seat. He is terrified and becomes disturbed. Lady Macbeth tries to explain his odd behaviour to the guests. He is not well, she says, and then quietly tells him to be sensible. He is imagining things. She believes it is better if the guests leave. When they do, Macbeth soon recovers. But he insists on seeing the witches again as soon as he can.

19

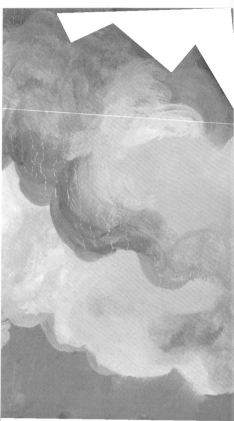

 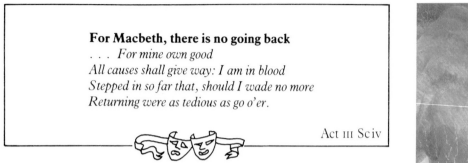
The witches foretell disaster

Macbeth finds the 'secret, black and midnight-hags' in a cave boiling up their witches' brew full of toads, snakes and other ghastly things. He demands that they tell him what is going to happen. They tell him to beware of Macduff. They say that no one 'of woman born' will harm Macbeth. Then they say he will not be defeated until 'Birnam wood comes to Dunsinane.' Macbeth is not too alarmed by these sayings. Anyway, he is convinced about the last one because forests and trees cannot move. Next he asks if Banquo's heirs will be kings. He is shown a vision of eight kings – which means that they will.

> **The witches' brew**
> Second Witch *Fillet of a fenny snake,*
> *In the cauldron boil and bake;*
> *Eye of newt and toe of frog,*
> *Wool of bat and tongue of dog,*
> *Adder's fork and blind-worm's sting,*
> *Lizard's leg and howlet's wing,*
> *For a charm of powerful trouble,*
> *Like a hell-broth boil and bubble.*
> All *Double, double toil and trouble;*
> *Fire burn and cauldron bubble.*
>
> Act IV Sc i

20

Macbeth's revenge on Macduff

Macbeth learns that Macduff has turned against him. He has fled to England to join Malcolm who is organising an army to march on Macbeth. In revenge he decides to kill Macduff's family. Lady Macduff, who is upset that her husband has hurried off to England, does not have time to flee. She and her children are brutally murdered.

Malcolm tests Macduff's loyalty

In England Malcolm at first does not trust Macduff. He thinks he could be a spy for Macbeth. So he tests his loyalty by describing his own faults. Malcolm paints an evil picture of himself and Macduff is shocked. Then Malcolm confesses he has lied; he just needed proof that Macduff was on his side. Macduff now learns that his wife and family have been killed by Macbeth. Grief stricken, he is determined to kill Macbeth himself.

Lady Macbeth sleepwalks

Back in Scotland, Lady Macbeth is behaving oddly. Her lady in waiting tells the doctor how her mistress sleepwalks. They watch as she walks, talking to herself about Duncan's murder and rubbing her hands. In her mind she describes what happened and tries to wash the blood from her hands over and over again. Her guilt has driven her mad.

Lady Macbeth sleepwalking

*Out, damned spot! out, I say! . . . who would
have thought the old man to have had so much blood in
him? . . . What, will these hands ne'er be clean . . . Here's
the smell of blood still: all the perfumes of Arabia
will not sweeten this little hand . . .*

Act v Sci

22

Macbeth prepares for battle

Macbeth, however, is busy setting up defences all around Dunsinane Castle. Most of his noblemen and soldiers have joined the other side. But he is certain he cannot be beaten – or not until Birnam forest comes to Dunsinane.

What he does not know is that his enemies have agreed to meet at Birnam wood. When the soldiers are gathered there, each one is given the branch of a tree to camouflage them as they move forward to attack. As he is preparing for battle, Macbeth hears that Lady Macbeth has killed herself. Now alone, he thinks how meaningless life is. Just then, a messenger announces that Birnam wood appears to move.

Macbeth on how meaningless life is

To-morrow, and to-morrow, and to-morrow,
Creeps in this petty pace from day to day,
To the last syllable of recorded time;
And all our yesterdays have lighted fools
The way to dusty death. Out, out, brief candle!
Life's but a walking shadow, a poor player
That struts and frets his hour upon the stage,
And then is heard no more: it is a tale
Told by an idiot, full of sound and fury,
Signifying nothing.

Act v Sc v

When Birnam wood meets Dunsinane

Malcolm and Macduff have begun their attack. And for Macbeth, the witches' prophecy has come true. Macbeth fights bravely but his castle is taken. He meets Macduff on the battlefield but still believes he cannot be killed by a man 'of woman born'. But Macduff reveals that he was born prematurely by Caesarian – so he was not born in the normal way. And in their fight Macbeth is killed. Now at last peace is restored to Scotland and the rightful heir, Malcolm, is crowned king.

The play's characters

Lady Macbeth's accusation of cowardice
. . . Would'st thou have that
Which thou esteem'st the ornament of life,
And live a coward in thine own esteem,
Letting 'I dare not' wait upon 'I would'

Act 1 Sc vii

Macbeth

Macbeth is one of the most complicated of Shakespeare's characters. In describing him, Shakespeare shows how well he understands how different people think and act – and how a person can be driven to evil deeds by hidden ambitions and emotions within themselves.

At the beginning of the play, we learn that Macbeth is a brave soldier and a good man. He has proved his loyalty to King Duncan by defeating the enemy. Only after he meets the witches does he begin to think evil thoughts. But, being a good man, at first he does not give in to these.

Lady Macbeth knows her husband's nature better than most other people. She knows that deep down he wants to be king, just as the witches prophesied. But she thinks he is too weak willed to do anything about it. She realises that she must be the person who urges him to kill Duncan. And she does. This shows how easily swayed Macbeth is, as does his listening to the witches in the first place.

Macbeth is not so worried about the wrong he is doing until after he has killed Duncan. Then he feels guilty and troubled by his conscience. He is in such a state of shock that he thinks he hears voices saying he has murdered sleep. But he soon puts these fears aside and pulls himself together.

When he becomes king, the evil side of his nature takes over completely. He becomes a butcher and a tyrant without any feelings of remorse. He plans the murder of Banquo in the most cold-blooded way. Before, he had to be persuaded by his wife to kill. Now, he does not even bother to tell her of his plans. We do get one glimpse of the cowardly side of his nature at the banquet when he is disturbed by the vision of Banquo's ghost. But as before, the feeling of fear and guilt soon passes. By now, he knows that he has given in to the evil.

He callously orders the brutal murder of Lady Macduff and her children even though they can do him no harm. Even when his wife goes mad, he does not show much concern. He trusts completely in the witches' prophecies. Although he is deserted by his soldiers and hated by everyone, he really believes he cannot be defeated.

Only when his wife commits suicide does he show some feeling. Then we see what kind of man he might have been had he not given in to evil. And just for a moment we feel sorry for him, as he thinks about how meaningless his life is – and about his hopes for a happy old age. His spirit is broken but he is determined to carry on. And in the end he dies bravely. What is tragic in this story, Shakespeare tells us, is that here was a good, honest and honourable man who allowed himself to be totally corrupted by evil ambitions.

Macbeth's ambitions

Macbeth . . . *Stars, hide your*
    fires!
Let not light see my black and
    deep desires . . .

                                Act I Sc iv

Macbeth on the murder of Duncan

If it were done, when 'tis done,
    then 'twere well
It were done quickly:

                                Act I Sc vii

Macduff's description of Macbeth

. . . Not in the legions
Of horrid hell can come a devil
    more damned
In evils to top Macbeth

                                Act IV Sc iii

No comfortable old age for Macbeth

. . . that which should
    accompany old age,
As honour, love, obedience,
    troops of friends,
I must not look to have

                                Act V Sc iii

Macbeth

Lady Macbeth dismisses failure
We fail?
But screw your courage to the sticking-place,
And we'll not fail . . .

Act I Sc vi

Lady Macbeth

Shakespeare deliberately creates a contrast between the nature of Lady Macbeth and her husband. At the beginning of the play, she is the strong-willed, ambitious person. It is Macbeth who is weak and uncertain. But, like Macbeth, Shakespeare shows us how her character is affected by the murders of Duncan and Banquo so that she goes mad and commits suicide.

Lady Macbeth is more ambitious for her husband than he is. She imagines a wonderful future for him as king. Only for a moment does she stop to think if it is right or wrong to kill Duncan. She expresses her feelings so strongly that Macbeth – who is rather a weak person – totally gives in to her wishes. She is also a sensible and practical woman. She plans the details of the murder. And she drugs the guards and puts out the daggers. When Macbeth is too shaken to return the daggers after the murder, she does it.

She, then, is the wicked woman who goads Macbeth into murdering Duncan. Without her Macbeth might not have translated the temptation to murder into the actual deed. Remember, though, that Lady Macbeth is not only ambitious for herself – but also for Macbeth. In this respect, she is a good wife who supports her husband's plans for getting on in the world. She is a charming hostess to Duncan and later at the banquet apologises for Macbeth's strange behaviour. She is self-confident and calm whenever Macbeth panics or imagines things. She knows Macbeth's weak points. And she uses her own strong nature to supply the courage he does not have. (In other circumstances, you might almost admire her tremendous determination to get for Macbeth what he wants.) She certainly cannot count on her husband when her courage deserts her. Once Macbeth becomes king he does not need

Lady Macbeth's determination to kill Duncan

. . . Come, thick Night,
And pall thee in the dunnest smoke of Hell,
That my keen knife see not the wound it makes,
Nor Heaven peep through the blanket of the dark,
To cry, 'Hold, hold!'

Act I Sc v

his wife's support. It is as if her strength of character has been taken over by him – and his weaknesses by her.

She is now the person who broods about the dreadful things they have done. She is frightened of the dark. She walks in her sleep and washes her hands all the time to get rid of the blood. Her guilty conscience drives her mad and she commits suicide.

Duncan

Shakespeare uses the character of Duncan to make a contrast with Macbeth. While Macbeth is a traitor, Duncan is honest, humble and good. He shows he has a generous nature by praising Macbeth so warmly and by giving Lady Macbeth the present of a diamond. Popular with his subjects, he ruled fairly and wisely. By murdering him, Shakespeare tells us, Macbeth murdered an ideal king.

Duncan

Banquo

Like Macbeth, Banquo is a brave and loyal soldier. When he is with Macbeth and the witches he too is given a prophecy. But he recognises that the witches are evil creatures and he resists their temptations. He is an honest and trusting man and he does not suspect Macbeth until it is too late. In a way, Banquo is the hero of the play. Whereas Macbeth gives in to evil thoughts and ambitions, Banquo does not. And this, Shakespeare is telling us, is how Macbeth should have acted.

Macduff

Macduff is suspicious of Macbeth straight after Duncan's murder. Like Banquo, he is a straightforward, honest man. He firmly believes that the tyrant Macbeth must be destroyed and the rightful king, Malcolm, put on the throne. He is a man of action and goes to England to join Malcolm. But this brave act causes the death of his unprotected wife and children. He gets his revenge, however, by killing Macbeth and helping to restore peace to Scotland.

Macduff on the death of his family

I cannot but remember such things were,
That were most precious to me. Did heaven look on,
And would not take their part? Sinful Macduff,
They were all struck for thee! . . .

Act IV Sc iv

Banquo   Macduff

The life and plays of Shakespeare

Life of Shakespeare

1564 William Shakespeare born at Stratford-upon-Avon.

1582 Shakespeare marries Anne Hathaway, eight years his senior.

1583 Shakespeare's daughter, Susanna, is born.

1585 The twins, Hamnet and Judith, are born.

1587 Shakespeare goes to London.

1591-2 Shakespeare writes *The Comedy of Errors*. He is becoming well-known as an actor and writer.

1592 Theatres closed because of plague.

1593-4 Shakespeare writes *Titus Andronicus* and *The Taming of the Shrew*: he is member of the theatrical company, the Chamberlain's Men.

1594-5 Shakespeare writes *Romeo and Juliet*.

1595 Shakespeare writes *A Midsummer Night's Dream*.

1595-6 Shakespeare writes *Richard II*.

1596 Shakespeare's son, Hamnet, dies. He writes *King John* and *The Merchant of Venice*.

1597 Shakespeare buys New Place in Stratford.

1597-8 Shakespeare writes *Henry IV*.

1599 Shakespeare's theatre company opens the Globe Theatre.

1599-1600 Shakespeare writes *As You Like It*, *Henry V* and *Twelfth Night*.

1600-01 Shakespeare writes *Hamlet*.

1602-03 Shakespeare writes *All's Well That Ends Well*.

1603 Elizabeth I dies. James I becomes king. Theatres closed because of plague.

1603-04 Shakespeare writes *Othello*.

1605 Theatres closed because of plague.

1605-06 Shakespeare writes *Macbeth* and *King Lear*.

1606-07 Shakespeare writes *Antony and Cleopatra*.

1607 Susanna Shakespeare marries Dr John Hall. Theatres closed because of plague.

1608 Shakespeare's granddaughter, Elizabeth Hall, is born.

1609 *Sonnets* published. Theatres closed because of plague.

1610 Theatres closed because of plague. Shakespeare gives up his London lodgings and retires to Stratford.

1611-12 Shakespeare writes *The Tempest*.

1613 Globe Theatre burns to the ground during a performance of Henry VIII.

1616 Shakespeare dies on 23 April.

Shakespeare's plays

The Comedy of Errors
Love's Labour's Lost
Henry VI Part 2
Henry VI Part 3
Henry VI Part 1
Richard III
Titus Andronicus
The Taming of the Shrew
The Two Gentlemen of Verona
Romeo and Juliet
Richard II
A Midsummer Night's Dream
King John
The Merchant of Venice
Henry IV Part 1
Henry IV Part 2
Much Ado About Nothing
Henry V
Julius Caesar
As You Like It
Twelfth Night
Hamlet
The Merry Wives of Windsor
Troilus and Cressida
All's Well That Ends Well
Othello
Measure for Measure
King Lear
Macbeth
Antony and Cleopatra
Timon of Athens
Coriolanus
Pericles
Cymbeline
The Winter's Tale
The Tempest
Henry VIII

Index

Numerals in *italics* refer to picture captions.

Acknowledgements

The publishers would like to thank Morag
Gibson for her help in producing this book.

Picture credits

p. 1 Governors of Royal Shakespeare
Theatre, Stratford-upon-Avon, p. 5
Bridgeman Art Library (reproduced by
permission of Viscount De L'Isle VC, KG
from his private collection, p. 6 NPG.